To Fulfil, Not to Destroy

To Fulfil, Not to Destroy

Christ as the Fulfilment of Hindu Religious Experience in Indian Christian Theology

Ivan M. Satyavrata

regnum
Mini Book Series

Edited by David Cranston

First published 2018 by Regnum Books International

Regnum is an imprint of the Oxford Centre for Mission Studies
St. Philip and St. James Church
Woodstock Road, Oxford OX2 6HR, UK
www.ocms.ac.uk/regnum

09 08 07 06 05 04 03 7 6 5 4 3 2 1

British Library Cataloguing in Publication Data. A catalogue record for this book is available from the British Library.

ISBN: 978-1-506476-88-9

eBook ISBN: 978-1-506476-89-6

Typeset in Candara by Words by Design.

The publication of this volume is made possible through the kind financial assistance of EMW (Evangelisches Missionswerk).

Distributed by 1517 Media in the US and Canada

For Sheila, Rohan, Rahul & Phengsy
Life's dearest treasures
God's greatest gifts
My joy and reward

Foreword

From Abraham's conversation with Melchizedek to Paul's speech in Athens, the Bible portrays many encounters between people who knew the living God in the context of his covenant revelation, and others who stood on different ground and yet are presented as having some knowledge of God and some impulse to seek after God and worship him. What are we to make of such encounters, and how are we to envisage the spiritual reality that lies behind them, and articulate the relationship between their pre-existing religious understandings and the faith declared to them in the name of the biblical God, founded on his words and deeds climaxing in Jesus Christ?

Substitute the small governing council of Athens, heirs to the few centuries of Greek religion and philosophy that formed the worldview from which they listened to Paul, for the millions of Indians over countless generations whose worldview has been shaped for two millennia by the philosophy and religion of the Vedas and other scriptures of what was eventually categorised as 'Hinduism', and one begins to see the scale of the task confronting Christian mission in that land through the centuries.

The Bible affirms two great truths, as integral and essential to each other as the dynamic relationship of breathing in and breathing out. There is the universality of the Bible's teaching about humanity, and there is the particularity of the Bible's teaching about God's revealing and saving action in and through Jesus of Nazareth.

How then does the one hand relate to the other hand? When people come out of a religious tradition that contains elements of truth and revelation alongside the marks of human ignorance and sin, and meet the living God in and through encounter with Jesus Christ and put their faith in him – how are they (or we) to express the relationship between their Christ-centred faith and their prior religious understanding and practice? That has been a divisive issue of Christian mission from the very beginning which can be seen in the conflict between Christian believers from Jewish and Gentile backgrounds in the New Testament itself.

This book, a concise version of Dr Satyavrata's doctoral work as a distinguished Langham Scholar, explores a significant strand of Christian theologising on this issue associated with the word 'fulfilment'. From having been a major and influential way of articulating the relationship in the early twentieth century, it has suffered neglect more recently, particularly in evangelical missiology and missionary practice. His thorough analysis of three major figures in Indian Christian history and their antecedents is richly illuminating and he articulates a theologically defensible synthesis of what we can learn from them in our generation. May this fruit of his own research bear more fruit among those who read and heed his work.

Christopher J.H. Wright
International Ministries Director
Langham Partnership

Glossary

Advaita Vedanta

A Hindu school of philosophy and religious practice, and one of the classic Indian paths to spiritual realisation.

Bhagavad Gita

A 700-verse Hindu scripture in Sanskrit, which taught an undivided devotedness to God, and an aspiration for giving up the world and practising humility and forbearance.

Bhakti

The *Bhakti* movement refers to the theistic devotional trend that emerged in mediaeval Hinduism and later revolutionised Sikhism. It originated in eighth century Tamil South India, now part of Tamilnadu and Kerala, and spread northwards. *Bhakti* literally means attachment, participation, homage, faith, love, devotion, worship and purity. In Hinduism, it refers to devotion to, and love for, a personal god. The *Bhakti* tradition from the root *bhaj-* means service, worship, loyalty and loving devotion to God.

Brahmin

The Brahmins are a Hindu caste specialising as priests, teachers and protectors of sacred learning across the generations. The Chitpavan Brahmin is a Hindu Brahmin community inhabiting Konkan, the coastal region of the state of Maharashtra in India.

Fulfilment theology

Fulfilment theology is based on a theory of the relationship between Christianity and other religions, which holds that all religious traditions have partial access to the truth, to spirituality and to transcendence, but Christianity has access to them in all their fulness.

Karma

The law of karma refers to the spiritual principle of cause and effect where the intent and actions of an individual (the cause) influence the future of that individual (the effect), and can be summed up as 'I am what I am because of what I was, and what I am won't make any difference to what I was but only what I might be'.

Logos

The Logos is the agent and sustainer of the created world, present and active in it since the time of creation.

Pantheism

The belief that God is not personal, that the universe is identical with divinity, and that everything resides in an all-encompassing and immanent God.

Saccidananda

The ultimate, unchanging reality.

Sadhu

Derived from the route *sadh-* which means 'directing to the goal', the term *Sadhu* commonly denotes the Hindu ascetic or holy man who follows a definite way of life or discipline adopted in order to attain an immediate experience of the divine.

Sanskrit is an ancient Indian language. It is a sacred language of Hinduism, Buddhism and Jainism, as well as the origin of many of the Indian languages.

Vaishnavism is one of the major traditions within the broader Vedic, or Hindu, spiritual culture. Unlike some Vedic traditions, *Vaishnavas* believe that the ultimate reality is personal. They thus understand that God is the Supreme, all-attractive person, of whom Krishna is a manifestation. They acknowledge that all living beings are eternal persons.

Vedas

The Vedas are a large body of knowledge texts originating in the ancient Indian subcontinent. Composed in Vedic Sanskrit, the texts constitute the oldest layer of Sanskrit literature and the oldest scriptures of Hinduism

Contents

Introduction to This Edition

The Christian Church has always had to address the question of how much common ground there may be between the Christian faith and other religions. While the issue not new, the relationship has come to occupy a more prominent position in the modern world of theological reflection. In the two-thirds world, with its struggle for social harmony amidst growing religious fundamentalism, the issue has critical personal, social, political and academic consequences.

The fundamental question can be stated as follows: "Is there a way of relating the Christian faith and experience to other religions, which ascribes genuine value to the religious experience of people of other faiths, while affirming the essential claims of the Christian faith?"

Evangelical Christians, with a narrow focus and a firm commitment to active missionary engagement, tend to focus on the uniqueness of Christ. Pluralists, on the other hand, with broader views, often respond in ways that seem to compromise the integrity of the Christian tradition.

Christianity did not come into a religious vacuum but into a world of living religions. Wherever the Christian faith went, there was already an existing religious tradition. The original membership of the Church consisted of converts from different religions, and over the centuries as the Christian Gospel spread to new lands, vast numbers of people of diverse backgrounds, cultures and religions responded to the Gospel and became members of the Church. This book is a condensation of Ivan Satyavrata's doctoral thesis carried out at the Oxford Centre for Mission Studies examining these issues in his national Indian context.

Introduction

The Christian tradition in India has had many converts to the Christian faith, in whom the tension between their new-found allegiance to Christ and love for their ancestral tradition was profound. Several of them found a satisfactory resolution to their struggle by regarding their new-found faith in Christ as in some way fulfilling the highest aspirations of their pre-Christian religious experience.

Fulfilment theology is based on a theory of the relationship between Christianity and other religions which holds that all religious traditions have partial access to the truth, to spirituality, and to transcendence, but Christianity has access to them in all their fulness.

This book focuses on this 'fulfilment stream', as it is called, as expressed in the experience of Indian Christian converts during the pre-Independence period of 1820-1947.

This was the time when Protestant missionary Christianity encountered Hinduism, and it represents an important era in which the relationship of Christianity to Hinduism was first raised and discussed. The origins of an authentic Indian Christian identity and theological tradition may be traced back to the pioneering efforts of the Indian converts of this period who offered creative and original insights into the fundamental issues in the Christian-Hindu encounter. A number of fulfilment approaches during this period will be considered to see how different scholars related the Christian faith to other religions in a way that both affirms the truths of Christianity while also ascribing genuine worth to other faiths.

The 'fulfilment concept' is defined in relation to three principal models which emerged at critical moments of significance in the Christian encounter with other traditions. First, in the emergence of the Gospel from its theological cradle, the Jewish faith. Secondly, in the early Church's encounter with Greek culture in the second and third centuries. Thirdly, in the nineteenth century Protestant missionary encounter with the religions of India.

It is important to recognise that the belief that Christianity fulfils other religions can be traced back, almost continuously, through the history of the Church, beginning with Jesus' attitude to Judaism. This is reflected in his words in Matthew 5 v 17: "Do not think that I have come to abolish the law and the prophets; I have come not to abolish them but to fulfil them."

Although in its original context, it applied primarily to the fulfilment of the Jewish Messianic expectations in the coming of Christ, a further application may be found in certain New Testament texts to other non-Christian cultures – for example, in the concept of the Logos in John chapter 1, in the address of Paul to Gentile audiences in Acts chapters 14 and 17, and in Paul's creation theology in Romans chapters 1 and 2. Furthermore, the early Church Fathers' approach to non-Christian philosophy and religion was also based on a fulfilment reading of the New Testament, recognising the Logos as the agent and sustainer of the created world, present and active in it since the time of creation,

For both Jew and Gentile alike, the Logos represented the ruling fact of the universe, the self-expression of God and the starting-point of all things. It was a term that would be widely recognised by a Gentile audience and would strike a familiar chord among Greek readers in particular. It is based on the prevailing understanding of the Logos as the self-expression of the ultimate divinity, which gave unity to the whole cosmos. The author of the fourth Gospel and some early patristic writers employed it in communicating the truth of the incarnation to the Greek world. The Church endorsed the specific Christian significance assigned to this term.

Looking at these models in a little more detail, we see a prophetic or promise fulfilment in Jesus' words in Matthew 5 v 17. This describes the approach of the first century Christians to Old Testament Judaism, based on the biblical concept of divine salvation history. Historically, Christianity has defined itself as the fulfilment of Judaism, and this is the most basic expression of the fulfilment theme, that the Messiah was promised, predicted, and prefigured in the Old Testament and that the incarnation, crucifixion and resurrection of Christ took place in fulfilment of the Old Testament predictions.

The second type of fulfilment is known as the 'Logos-historical' model. The early Church Fathers saw no other way in which humanity could come to know the transcendent God except through revelation by the 'Logos', as Christ is described in John chapter 1 – the Eternal Creator who is one with the Father. They were careful to distinguish the revelation recorded to the Jews through the Law from the light of nature present in Gentile philosophies, and the divine inspiration of the Old Testament prophets from the illuminating action of the Logos.

The clear expression of this model first emerged in the second and third centuries in the second defining moment of the Church's encounter with Greek culture. As the Church began to spread outside Palestine it was confronted by the challenge from the world of Greek philosophy and religion. The Christian movement was no longer just a Jewish sect, but a faith which claimed to be universal, complete with a missionary mandate. However, the questions became more complex. What part do non-Jewish religions have in the economy of God? Are there legitimate religious aspirations or valid points of contact in them? How were the claims of the Christian faith to be related to different forms of pre-Christian religion?

The earliest theologians of the Church formulated their attitude to non-Christian religions in terms of these questions, and the response generally took the form of uncompromising hostility to what was commonly regarded as paganism. However, we also find some of the most generous recognitions of the work of God outside the Church during this period. Although the early Fathers are the main source of reflection on this theme, it is based on their understanding of the Old and New Testaments. The Fathers sometimes treated Greek philosophy and literature as a type of Old Testament designating the elements of continuity and discontinuity within it by the respective terms 'preparation' and 'transcendence'. The essential challenge they seem to have faced was to hold these two elements together. They succeeded in their attempt to do so through their view of salvation history and their vision of the universal scope of God's purpose for humankind.

The third model is termed 'evolutionary fulfilment'. As its name suggests, this model was developed in the nineteenth century under the influence of Darwin's evolutionary theory, on the scientific study of religion. It recognises the presence of fragments of truth in all religions, and sees all the religions of the world as being in an evolutionary scheme of development. Within this, the lower religions are fulfilled by the higher religions, and most exponents of this model agree that Christianity is at the highest end of the continuum.

The sharp distinction between Christian and non-Christian salvation history is minimised in fulfilment approaches. This is done in various ways by emphasising the universality of God's cosmic covenant. Christianity is thus viewed as a cosmic religion in which the truths and values of all religions, as well as all human religious aspirations, can be incorporated. Christ is not just the Saviour of Christians, but of all people, and non-Christian religions are viewed as part of a theology of history orientated towards Christ as the universal Saviour.

All models of fulfilment accept the provisional nature of other religions with varying degrees of emphasis. All agree that these religions express human anticipation of something fuller, the fulness offered only in Christ. As Christ becomes known, he transforms, subsumes, and replaces all pre-Christian religions.

The Background and Development of the Protestant Fulfilment Tradition in the Nineteenth Century

The nineteenth century missionary movement opened up Protestant Christianity, previously restricted to Europe, to other regions of the world. The dominant position of the Protestant missionaries during this period was conservative and confrontational. However, a minority aimed at the more peaceful, or irenic, attitude in the closing decades of the nineteenth century, and this expressed itself in an increasingly influential fulfilment approach.

Nineteenth century Protestant missions were the outworking of the evangelical awakening in Britain. One of its deepest convictions was the ultimate lostness of the heathen, apart from Christ. It was perceived as a straightforward conflict between the revealed truth of God and false and idolatrous religious systems. The predominant attitude of British missionaries towards Indian religions was critical and denunciatory. William Wilberforce viewed the Hindu divinities as absolute monsters of injustice, wickedness and cruelty, and their religious system as an abomination. Although the missionaries were motivated by sincere intentions, their approach was restricted by the limitations of their theological framework and their fragmentary knowledge of Hinduism.

The Lutheran pioneer missionary, Bartholomaeus Ziegenbalg, in the early years of the eighteenth century, conducted a vigorous religious dialogue with learned members of the Hindu community and he was sympathetic to the Hindu tradition. He recognised the existence of common ground, and expressed positive appreciation for certain elements of truth found in the Hindu religious system.

There were, on the other hand, several non-theological factors which contributed to the perception of the confrontational missionary attitude in the nineteenth century. First, the problem of cultural imperialism which was implicit in the colonial education policy underlying the educational philosophy of some missionaries. Secondly, the 'mission compound mentality', which alienated the missionaries from the surrounding culture, and dissociated the convert from his cultural roots. Thirdly, the growing success of the Christian mission among the lower castes and outcasts which were remote from the Hindu social structure. This limited encounters between Christians and Hindu scholars, and reinforced negative attitudes towards Hinduism. Fourthly, conservative attitudes in the western churches meant that mission agencies were largely ignorant of the Hindu religion.

It is important not to generalise about the situation. The East India Company had for a long time maintained a policy of cautious tolerance towards both Hinduism and Islam, and even accepted and supported these religions, and indeed not all the Protestant missionaries of this period viewed Hinduism with contempt.

Oriental scholars respected the belief in the essential cultural unity of all humankind based on common origins. But the perception that Christianity was a denationalising force was fuelled by a new-found pride in India's past, and this intensified Hindu resistance to the Christian missionary assault and strengthened the forces of religious and political nationalism. The missionaries faced their strongest opposition from educated Hindus. The growing frustration with the failure of the confrontational approach to evangelise the Hindu compelled the Protestant missionaries to re-evaluate their traditional attitudes.

Meanwhile, in Europe, the influence of the evolutionary hypothesis was beginning to give rise to a more sympathetic attitude to Hinduism. The 1890s saw the introduction of the study of comparative religions in many of the seminaries and universities in the west. However, despite this, the peaceful, irenic, view remained in the minority, waiting for broader acceptance of the fulfilment approach in the early years of the twentieth century.

The Emergence of the Protestant Missionary Fulfilment Approach

The original ideas leading to the emergence of the Protestant fulfilment approach were expressed in the writings of four notable theologians: Richard Trench, Frederick Maurice, Rowland Williams and John Morris. The first three were influenced by the same Cambridge school of liberal theology, reflecting a similar openness to truth in other religions while, at the same time, affirming that all the nobler longings of the heathen world are satisfied in Christianity. In India, the British evangelical scholar, John Muir, encouraged missionaries to adopt a respectful and conciliatory attitude towards Indian culture based on his intimate knowledge of Hinduism. T.E. Slater, at the end of the nineteenth century, was the first evangelical missionary in India who tried to develop a fulfilment approach. He recognised traces of truth and excellence in Hindu scriptures. He felt that the missionary must have a detailed knowledge of Hinduism which would lead to an attitude of sympathy towards them. The verdict of the World Missionary Conference in Edinburgh in 1910 was that, for a large majority of missionaries, the fulfilment approach represented the most promising strategy for the completion of their missionary task. In this way, the positive attitude to other religions found growing acceptance as an alternative to the confrontational Protestant missionary position in the second half of the nineteenth century. While a prominent feature of these fulfilment approaches was the influence of the evolutionary theory, their main strength was that they were based on a rigorous study of the Hindu religious texts, and consolidated in practical inter-religious dialogues.

There were several important strands of Indian Christian thought related to the fulfilment approaches in the pre-Independence Indian context. First, each sought to penetrate the heart of the Christian faith as they had been deeply influenced by the person and message of Christ. Secondly, all shared a common non-Christian ancestry and responded to Christ with their religious and cultural roots deeply embedded within various Hindu traditions. Thirdly, all belonged to the high-caste Hindu community in India, and had their centre of gravity and thinking in the Sanskrit tradition. Four key thinkers will be discussed.

Keshub Chunder Sen (1838-84)

Sen was a key figure in the development of Indian Christian theology. Although he remained within the Hindu fold, he was nevertheless deeply attracted to Christianity. The formative influences on his life were *Vaishnava Bhakti* with its yogic mysticism, and devotion to Christ, apart from the western trappings of organised Christianity.

Vaishnavism is one of the major traditions within the broader Vedic, or Hindu, spiritual culture. Unlike some Vedic traditions, *Vaishnavas* believe that the ultimate reality is personal. The *Bhakti* movement refers to the theistic devotional trend that emerged in mediaeval Hinduism, and expresses religious devotion in terms of an intimate relationship between the human being and a personal God based on mutual love.

Sen saw Christ as having come to fulfil what was best in all the world's religions. He viewed the Hindu tradition in much the same way as a Jewish Christian would regard the Old Testament, perceiving no qualitative distinction between the Old Testament Hebrew and Hindu dispensations, both of which he saw fulfilled in Christ.

He was less concerned with the historical person of Christ than with the pre-existent Logos. He refers to what he calls the larger 'spirit-Christ' (John 1) as opposed to the 'smaller' Christ of Nazareth. His view of Christ is accordingly not exclusive, but all-inclusive, and he appeals to the testimony of the Church Fathers in support of this view of the all-pervading and eternal Logos-Christ. Whereas the early Church Fathers saw the Logos-Christ firmly grounded in the 'smaller' Christ of history, the bedrock of Sen's religious faith is not the Christ of history, but the Logos-Christ of mystical experience, present in every human heart.

He saw Christ as already present in every true Brahmin and in every Hindu as the Holy Word or the eternal Veda. Sen challenges his hearers to experience Christ as the 'Light that lighted every man that cometh into the world'. The climax of this continued evolution of the Logos is Jesus Christ. Sen's fulfilment approach is a genuine attempt to respond to the person and message of Christ from within the Hindu religious and cultural framework.

Nehemiah Goreh (1825-95)

The nineteenth century witnessed the conversion to Christ of a number of educated Hindus who helped to shape indigenous Indian Christian identity. Nehemiah Goreh was a high-caste Brahmin by birth and a Sanskrit scholar of outstanding stature. The Brahmins specialised as priests, teachers and protectors of sacred learning across the generations and Goreh's early years of training as a Chitpavan Brahmin took place in Benares on the banks of the Ganges in Uttar Pradesh in North India, a place regarded as the spiritual capital of India. Chitpavans have played a key role in the history of India over the centuries.

In his magnum opus, *A rational refutation of the Hindu philosophical systems*, Goreh displays a negative attitude towards Hinduism. However, he loves his fellow countrymen, is at home in their society, and was convinced that, in some unknown way, God had been preparing their hearts and minds to receive the Christian revelation. In two of his later works he acknowledges the possibility that these false religions contained some elements of the truth. He believed that the Bhagavad Gita, a 700-verse Hindu scripture in Sanskrit, which taught an undivided devotedness to God, and an aspiration for giving up the world and practising humility and forbearance, enabled an appreciation of the Christian faith.

In this way, Goreh views Christ as the fulfilment of the anticipations and yearnings of his Hindu ancestors. Christians and Hindus share the belief that the highest goal of man is union with God, but the conviction that God alone can make provision for salvation is distinctively Christian.

Brahmabandhab Upadhyay (1861-1907)

Brahmabandhab Upadhyay was a disciple of Sen, and a Bengali Hindu Brahmin by birth. He became a member of the Roman Catholic Church while retaining his firm allegiance to both Hindu culture and Roman Catholicism. He viewed himself as Hindu as far as his physical and mental constitution went, but as a Catholic in regard to his immortal soul, and called himself a Hindu Catholic.

Upadhyay was from the Advaita Vedanta school of Hindu philosophy and religious practice. It is one of the classic Indian paths to spiritual realisation, and was dismissed as a form of pantheism by Christian thinkers in the early years of the nineteenth century. This philosophical school regards everything as residing in an all-encompassing, immanent God, and the individual soul is no different from Brahman, the supreme Cosmic Spirit in Hinduism.

Upadhyay consciously sought points of agreement between the Vedas, the oldest scriptures of Hinduism, and the Old Testament, but had no intention of supplanting the authority of the Old Testament with that of the Vedas. He responded to Christ as a person deeply rooted in his Hindu tradition, and found his experience and identity as a Hindu Christian most adequately expressed in the fulfilment approach.

N.V. Tilak (1862-1919)

Narayan Tilak was a Chitpavan Brahmin convert and a famous Maharashtrian poet. Passionately devoted to Christ and deeply committed to his Hindu spiritual heritage, he did his best to dispel the misconception that becoming a Christian involved denying one's traditional cultural heritage and separating oneself from the Hindu community.

Tilak was a proponent of the *Bhakti* School of Hinduism, which held a great attraction for Indian Christians because of its conception of God as a loving, personal being, One who is distinct from creation, bestows grace upon his creatures, and can be worshipped with feelings of deep love and personal devotion. He cautioned Christian missionaries against imposing a foreign version of the Christian faith in India, and advised them to show respect to the ancient religious traditions and sages of India. He respected all the world's saints as prophets of God, and held the belief that the sayings of the Hindu saints form the first 'Old Testament' for Hindus. His described his conversion as coming to the feet of Christ over the bridge of Tukaram, a seventeenth century poet-saint of the *Bhakti* movement in Maharashtra.

Tilak's positive attitude to the Hindu tradition is balanced by his clear conviction of God's revelation in Christ. He said that Hindus must be invited to accept Christ, not as the supplanter of their spiritual heritage but as its fulfilment. Towards the closing years of his life he made a break with the established church, launching an indigenous Christian movement called *Devacha Darbar*, or the Royal Court of God, a brotherhood of the baptised and unbaptised disciples of Christ.

In summary, Sen was almost certainly the first within the Indian context to have used the term 'fulfilment' to describe the relationship of Christ to other religions. Upadhyay, on the other hand, took Sen's original proposal in a Christocentric direction.

Goreh's apologetic approach is at the opposite end of the spectrum from Sen's, and the absolute decisiveness of Christ is clearly his starting-point. His concept of fulfilment is a tentative attempt to build a bridge from the light of God in general revelation within Hinduism, to acceptance of the full revelation of God in Christ Jesus. He was convinced that this is the bridge that must be crossed if the Hindu is to experience the fulfilment of the anticipations and longings of the religion of his birth. While the universal Logos-Christ is basic to Sen's view, Goreh grounds his conception of Logos, like the early Church Fathers, in the Christ of history.

While Tilak's theological orientation is similar to Goreh, his *bhakti* orientation and deeper Christian appropriation of the Hindu cultural tradition sets him apart. His coming to faith is the culmination of his spiritual journey along the path of the poet-saints of India, and his adoption of their devotional framework.

It is possible to demonstrate some western influence on Sen and Goreh. However, they had a fundamental desire to keep their pre-Christian cultural roots intact, and in this respect these approaches can be legitimately regarded as an indigenous development, rather than an induced imperialistic response.

The Fulfilment Model in John Farquhar's 'The Crown of Hinduism'

A more peaceful, harmonious attitude of Christian missionaries towards other religions began to grow in influence with the dawn of the twentieth century. Nowhere is this more evident or better exemplified then in the work of the Scottish missionary to India, John Nicol Farquhar.

Farquhar was born in Scotland, in Aberdeen in 1861, and was brought up as a member of the Evangelical Union which had its roots in Scottish Protestant Congregationalism. Converted to Christ at the age of 24, he began his studies at school in Aberdeen and completed them at Oxford University.

In 1891 Farquhar arrived in India as a lay educational missionary for the London Missionary Society, and began to teach at Bhowanipur, Calcutta, where he remained for eleven years. He was never ordained and in 1902 joined the staff of the Indian Young Men's Christian Association in order to devote more time to evangelistic work, first as national student secretary and later as literary secretary, a post he held until 1923. During these years he wrote several important books, notably *The Crown of Hinduism* (1913) and *Modern Religious Movements in India* (1915).

Farquhar left India in 1923 because of ill health, spending the last six years of his life as Professor of Comparative Religion in the University of Manchester where he died in 1929.

Farquhar was a prolific writer and became convinced that the most effective instrument for presenting Christ to the educated Hindu, in what was then a hostile environment, was apologetic literature sympathetic to the cultural heritage of India. His publication of the *Crown of Hinduism* was a sympathetic and highly positive Christian approach to Hinduism. Although his principal aspiration was an uncompromising loyalty to Christ and the Gospel, he was an educated missionary who was able to provide the educated Hindu a 'value-free' intellectual framework which he hoped would eventually challenge their traditional religious beliefs and cultures. When he arrived in India, religious and political nationalism was on the rise, and after 1905 the atmosphere became more antagonistic towards Christian mission. The need for a peaceful approach that would remove the cultural hindrances and lead to the favourable reception of the Christian faith in India, was strongly needed.

Farquhar based his Christian defence on the two main principles undergirding the scientific study of religion: the essential unity of the human race, and the understanding that human life is in an organic process of development.

His vision was always Christ-centred, but in an article entitled *Is Christianity the only true religion?* he wrote: "Christianity acknowledges... that God has spoken in many religions, and recognises that Christ is the light that lighted every man that cometh into the world."

And it is in this article that he introduces the term 'fulfilment' for the first time in his writings, and argues that, rightly read, the Bhagavad Gita is a clearly expressed prophecy of Christ.

Farquhar remained convinced, despite some false and even immoral forms of expression, that these instincts prepared Hindus to receive the full light of Christian truth and ones to which an appeal should be made in Gospel presentations. He asserted that every important Christian truth is foreshadowed in Hinduism although buried in heaps of rubbish. The task of the Christian worker is to discover these and indicate how they are fulfilled in Christ. He insists that a sympathetic attitude is an essential prerequisite for a proper understanding of Hinduism.

In 1910 he clarified his understanding of fulfilment further, arguing that the greatness of Hinduism offers a philosophical justification for it as a religion in its lofty theory of God and the world. Its sophisticated organisation, based on the authority of the Brahmins, its divine quality, and the inspiration of the Vedas and other sacred literature, contribute to making Hinduism one of the greatest religions in the world.

The Crown of Hinduism carries forward the argument by explaining how Christianity could become the one religion of India, without destroying its national, cultural or religious heritage. Although Farquhar anticipates the eventual collapse of Hinduism as a system, he remains convinced that the rich religious literary tradition of India would always continue to nurture and sustain the people of India.

He argues that an Indian Christianity of the future will incorporate within its framework a reborn Hinduism, emerging from a Christ-centred reinterpretation of the Hindu tradition.

In 1910 Farquhar published *Christ and the Religions of the World*, primarily for a British audience. He explains his understanding of the way in which Christ fulfils the Old Testament, and uses that as a model for the relationship between the Christian faith and other religions. He argues that when the legitimate spiritual yearnings of Hinduism find their satisfaction and fulfilment in Christ, then – and only then – will all that the Hindu philosophers, saints and ascetics toiled for come alive. Hinduism must die into Christianity, in order that all that is good in Hinduism may live.

Thus Farquhar's fulfilment apologetic was driven by the search for a comprehensive and unifying theory of the relationship between Christianity and Hinduism, motivated by his desire to relate Christ to the deepest religious aspirations of India. He sought to give non-Christian religions their rightful place, while always affirming the incontestable supremacy of the Christian faith.

The Crown of Hinduism was Farquhar's response to the need for an effective apologetic approach to the Hindu which would remove the misconception that the Christian Gospel was anti-national and destructive of the Indian religious and cultural heritage. He describes how improved modern communications had contributed to a greater interest in other religions and the desire to share one's own religious treasures with people of other faiths.

The fact that non-Christian religions have led multitudes of men and women to God, and continue to enable a valid religious experience, is evidence that all possess some measure of truth. However, while Farquhar accepted the belief that all religions contain some measure of the truth, he denied the absolute claim that all these religions were true. Irreconcilable differences and fundamental contradictions between different religions were evidence of the superiority of some religions over others, and he always maintained that Christianity held the highest place.

He summarised his view in the following way: "We have already seen how Christ provides the fulfilment of each of the highest aspirations and aims of Hinduism... every ray of light which is visible in the greatest part of the religion reappears in Him set in healthy institutions and spiritual worship... in Him is focused every ray of light that shines in Hinduism. He is the Crown of the faith of India."

A Critical Analysis of Farquhar's Fulfilment Approach

We have already seen that fulfilment theology denotes the completion of fragments of truth which are found in other religions. An imperfect truth completed by a perfect truth, a full revelation of what had once been a partial revelation and the full radiance of what had once been but a partial glow. It is only in Christianity that these other religions are fulfilled, the truth completed, the fragments united, the meaning clarified, satisfying the basic human religious needs and instincts in Christ.

Christ fulfils Hinduism in three ways. First, by clarifying, correcting, supplementing and transforming the elements of truth that Hinduism legitimately affirms. Secondly, by satisfying every valid religious aspiration and instinct expressed in Hinduism. Thirdly, by inviting the Hindu to allow a reborn, Christ-centred Hinduism to replace his or her ancestral faith.

Farquhar's view met with a mixed response in India, with the most severe theological criticism coming from A.G. Hogg, a missionary contemporary of Farquhar's, who criticised his theory as unsustainable in the light of the true Hindu religious experience.

Hogg felt that, even among those who agreed with him, Farquhar's argument went beyond the limits of available evidence.

He made five objections which warrant serious consideration.

The first objection Hogg raised to Farquhar was that he was suggesting that Christ offered the solution to a need which Hinduism did not feel. He argued that, although Christian beliefs are able to arouse a yearning in some, which then only Christ is able to satisfy, the undisturbed Hindu consciousness does not seek fulfilment in Christ or Christianity.

The second objection that Hogg raised was that Farquhar made the evidence fit his theory. Hogg concedes that Christ does fulfil what is good in Hinduism, but he argued that Farquhar's view is far-fetched, in that he insists that accepting Christ leaves out so much of what was in Hinduism, and fulfils so much of what was never in Hinduism. A further objection was that Farquhar was increasingly drawn to an evolutionary philosophy, which seemed to undermine the Christian doctrine of revelation. His description of Christianity as the 'evolutionary crown' of Hinduism seemed to suggest that Hinduism would automatically evolve into Christianity, thus reducing religion to a purely natural process. The fourth objection Hogg made was that the Judæo-Christian fulfilment model cannot be applied to the Hindu-Christian relationship. While Christians may indeed affirm the grandeur and the dignity of India's religious efforts, in the final analysis, these have failed to lead India to the true knowledge of God. Finally, Hogg argues that the fulfilment approach reflects an attitude of condescension to the Hindu and his religion.

In summary, it should be said that Farquhar was the one individual most responsible for bringing about a decisive change in the thinking of Christians over their relationship to other faiths in the first quarter of the twentieth century. He deserves credit, not as the originator of the fulfilment approach, but for developing it into a tradition of encounter and dialogue. Two factors facilitated his contribution in this regard: first, his scholarship was persuasive, combining sympathy and scholarly depth. Secondly, his editorship of *The Inquirer* and other publications gave him the opportunity to influence academic opinion. He was grounded in, and sympathetic to, non-Christian religions in general and to Hinduism in particular. A further strength of his approach was that it provided an empirical and theological basis for a positive appreciation of Hinduism and other religions. He not only pointed out elements of objective truth in other religions, which Christians could celebrate, he also defined continuity between religions in terms of the evolutionary framework, and by his identification of the fundamental religious consciousness common to all religions.

Thirdly, Farquhar's approach was based on the New Testament fulfilment model of Jesus. He saw this in terms of the biblical concept of progressive revelation, and he was influenced to a lesser extent by the approach of the early Church Fathers. However, two weaknesses remain in his writings. First, there is no reference to the indigenous Indian fulfilment ideas as expressed by Sen, Goreh and Banerjea. Secondly, his view is overly pessimistic of the future of Hinduism, seeing no future in it and anticipating its disintegration and eventual demise, to be replaced by the Christian faith.

Farquhar's life-work was devoted to the premise that Christ was the answer to the total Hindu religious tradition and experience. He described his work in this regard as 'the work of a poorly equipped pioneer in a vast unexplored country'. In the rest of the study we attempt to build on his discoveries by drawing from the insights of two Indian converts.

Fulfilment in Krishna Mohan Banerjea's Vedic Theology

The analysis of Farquhar's fulfilment view provides the framework for the examination of the fulfilment approaches in two representative Indian thinkers, Krishna Mohan Banerjea and Sundar Singh. The first half of the nineteenth century witnessed the critical encounter between western ideas and the traditions of India. This resulted from the introduction of English education, together with the contact of British officials and missionaries with the educated Hindu class in Bengal. It gave rise to a vigorous movement for social, cultural and intellectual change, commonly characterised as the Bengal Renaissance in which Banerjea was a leading figure.

Krishna Mohan Banerjea was born in 1813 to a poor Kulin Brahmin family. These are Bengali Hindu Brahmins, who trace their origin to the five families of Kannauj who migrated to Bengal from Central India.

He was brought up in an atmosphere of strict religious orthodoxy fostered by his pious mother and maternal grandfather, who was an outstanding Sanskrit scholar. Banerjea was an early representative of a progressive class of high-caste Bengalis called the *bhadralok* who attempted to assimilate the western lifestyle of the British within the traditional Hindu culture, thus setting in motion a process of cultural transformation with far-reaching consequences for Indian society as a whole.

In 1824 Banerjea entered a Hindu college where he came under the influence of Derozio, a controversial Eurasian teacher, and this led to him becoming a leader in the radical youth movement, later known as Young Bengal. Banerjea was at the forefront of a campaign against Hindu orthodoxy launched through the pages of *The Enquirer*, one of a number of periodicals of which he was the editor. His association with this movement and its critical rejection of Hindu orthodoxy resulted in him having to leave home. During this process of stress and spiritual turmoil he came under the influence of Alexander Duff, the Scottish Presbyterian missionary educator, and became convinced of the truth of Christianity. His subsequent conversion and baptism in 1832 caused a great stir within the high-caste Hindu community of Calcutta.

Banerjea was baptised in the Scottish Presbyterian Church but then transferred allegiance to the Anglican Church and was ordained in 1839, becoming the first Indian to be given charge of an Episcopal Church in Bengal. In 1852 he was appointed as professor at Bishop's College, Calcutta, where he served until 1867. In 1876 he was elected a municipal commissioner for Calcutta and was awarded the honorary degree of Doctor of Law by Calcutta University for his contribution to Oriental literature and higher education. In 1885, the year of his death, the British government conferred on him the rank of Companion of the Indian Empire.

Banerjea was a Christian statesman, linguist, historian, social reformer and national civil rights leader. He knew at least ten languages, and his great intellect and breadth of learning enabled him to engage in a wide variety of scholarly pursuits. He was a leading figure amongst a special class of pioneers of indigenous Christian thought, and one of a number of educated Hindu converts who struggled to shape the Christian identity in a way that affirmed their cultural and national heritage while remaining true to their Christian faith.

Banerjea is widely regarded as the foremost Indian Christian apologist of this period, making his theological contribution at a time when the religious confrontation between Christianity and Hinduism was at its height. Four main groups were involved in the controversies that arose during this period: the young Bengal Liberals, the orthodox Hindu party, the Brahmo Samaj, a social Hindu monotheistic reform movement, and the Christian missionaries.

In his earliest speeches and writings Banerjea sought to expose the errors and weaknesses of Hinduism. Later he moved away from this negative position and took a more positive attitude to Christian-Hindu dialogue, emphasising continuity and fulfilment rather than points of disagreement.

Banerjea's early apologies were historical and philosophical enquiries in which he sought to challenge the rationality of Hinduism, and to affirm the reasonableness of the Christian faith. In order to defend Christianity against the criticism of its opponents and convince his fellow countrymen to accept Christianity, he affirmed what he found to be true in Hinduism, and courageously condemned what he had discovered to be false. Rather than appealing to the Bible as the primary standard of truth for Christians, he looked towards the elements of truth in 'the work of the Law written in the hearts of men' – that is to say, to the intuitive sense of right and wrong determined by the authoritative voice of conscience.

Banerjea was critical of the Hindu suggestion that Christianity is a foreign religion destructive of the Indian way of life, pointing out that the Hindu tradition itself upholds the idea that truth should be judged on its merits, regardless of its origin. He drew attention to the inherent inconsistency in some orthodox schools of Hindu philosophy by pointing out that the Vedas themselves testify against eternity in that they contain the names of persons and places not eternal.

A substantial portion of Banerjea's argument is directed towards exposing the Buddhist influence upon Brahminial Hinduism. He concludes a careful historical and philosophical analysis by arguing that the essential teachings of the Hindu philosophies have been borrowed from Buddhism.

Although at this stage his approach was decidedly negative, Banerjea remained respectful towards his Hindu colleagues, in contrast to the harsh and virulent rhetoric that characterised much of the missionary attitude of that time. While overtones of imperialism tainted missionary approaches, Banerjea addressed his Hindu colleagues as one of them, as one who had come from the same fold.

In his later dialogues, Banerjea began to look for meaningful convergence between Hinduism and the Christian faith, rather than trying to undermine Hinduism. He did this by discovering parallels between the Old Testament and the Vedas, and his thoughts during this period were first stated in *Arian Witness* and remained substantially the same throughout his subsequent writings.

The major challenge to Christianity during this period was its rejection on nationalist grounds, and Banerjea sought to refute that charge by demonstrating its direct continuity with the fundamental teachings of the Vedas. He realised that, to convince the educated Hindu community of the relevance of the Christian Gospel, he would have to show its relationship to the ancient religion and culture of India. He saw more hope in such a meeting-point in the Vedas than in the philosophical schools that developed later.

He offered evidence for the view that Vedic Hinduism acknowledges the existence of a supreme, unborn, eternal being who is far above heaven and earth, although known by a variety of names.

He concludes with the assertion that Christianity is, in essence, a Vedic doctrine in its legitimately developed form, and therefore no person can be a true Hindu without being a Christian. His final impassioned appeal invites Hindu readers to consider his message as the voice of their ancestors.

His approach is one of the earliest attempts, by a Hindu convert, to relate his Christian faith to his ancestral religion. He is concerned to redeem the Christian faith from the charge of foreignness, and he demonstrates that Hindu converts could pledge allegiance to Christ while remaining loyal to their ancestral culture. In comparison with western missionaries, his approach was sensitive and reflected a sympathetic and sophisticated grasp of the Hindu religious tradition.

He devoted his endeavours to finding points of continuity between the Christian faith and the Hindu religious tradition, eventually finding a basis in the Vedas for an evangelistic appeal to Hindus.

The Vedic figure of *Prajapati* is crucial to Banerjea's promise-fulfilment scheme. *Prajapati*, the Vedic Hindu deity and Lord of creatures, is the figure who strides across the bridge that he tries to build between Christianity and Hinduism. He highlights the close parallels with the pre-existing Christ as Logos, the Lord or supporter of creation, *Purusha*, the Universal Principle that is eternal and indestructible, and the Hindu god *Viswakarma*, the author of the universe who, as half-mortal and half-immortal, he identified with the Universal Godhead. The most striking analogy, however, is in the representation of *Prajapati* as the divine self-sacrificer, and the divine saviour, through whose death, death itself is vanquished.

Prajapati thus prefigures and is fulfilled in the biblical description of Christ as God and man, mortal and immortal, who offered himself as a sacrifice for man's salvation from sin.

Banerjea argued that *Prajapati* corresponded with the Old Testament conception of a promised Messiah, which Jewish Christians saw fulfilled in the person of Jesus of Nazareth. However, he also seems to allow the figure of *Prajapati* to serve, in India, as a functional equivalent of the 'unknown God' in Paul's Athenian address, or the concept of the Logos in John's Gospel. Banerjea's approach bears some resemblance to that of the early Church Fathers and their attitude to Greek philosophy. Clement of Alexandria, for instance, clearly perceived certain fragments of truth in Greek philosophy as having an educational value for the Greeks, similar to that of the Law for the Jews. But while Clement regarded Greek philosophy as a way leading to Christ, he carefully distinguished the action of the Logos in Greek philosophy from the inspiration of the Hebrew prophets. Thus, just as the early Church Fathers saw certain fragments of truth in Greek philosophy, so Banerjea sees the same in his reading of the Vedas. Although he took the Vedas very seriously, he did not treat them on a par with the Christian Scriptures, but acknowledged germs or fragments of truth within them which agreed with Christian doctrine describing them as containing 'Fragments of diamonds sparkling amidst dust and mud'.

Banerjea's work seemed to be received enthusiastically by his contemporaries, and there is evidence to show that his writings were not only widely known but also met with favourable acceptance in some scholarly circles. For the most part they went unchallenged by Christian missionaries within, and the Hindu scholarly community without.

In summary, Banerjea was a product of his generation but also a thinker ahead of his time. His apologetic approach may have been conditioned by the theories that were exciting the intellectual world of his day, but the originality of his fulfilment approach marks it as a significant milestone in the history of the Christian-Hindu encounter. He was representative of a wider group of nineteenth- and twentieth century converts to Christianity, who tried to reinterpret their pre-Christian Hindu tradition from the perspective of their subsequent experience of Christ. There were significant differences in each approach, but all viewed their acceptance of the Christian faith as in some way a fulfilment of the Hindu religious experience.

Fulfilment in Sundar Singh's *Bhakti* Spirituality

Sundar Singh was born in 1889 in the village of Rampur in the Punjab, in north west India, into a wealthy landowner's family. They belonged to the high-caste Jat Sikh community, but both the Hindu and Sikh traditions had a formative influence on his life. He was the youngest son in the family and closely attached to his mother, a refined and deeply pious lady, who exercised a significant influence upon his early life by her own example and religious teaching in the Hindu and Sikh scriptures.

He came into contact with Christianity through Bible lessons at the American Presbyterian Mission primary school which he attended, and although he was outwardly resistant to Christianity, the teaching on the love of God had a great attraction for him. His deep spiritual thirst led him to search the Sikh Scriptures, or Granth, as well as the Qur'an and the sacred books of the Hindus. But all of them failed to satisfy his spiritual hunger. After the death of his mother and older brother, his spiritual crisis intensified, and initially manifested itself in violent opposition to the Christian faith, leading him to burn part of the New Testament. During this time he was getting up at three in the morning and praying for God to reveal himself and show him the way of salvation, and if that did not happen, he said he would commit suicide. One day he waited until 4:30 am expecting to see Buddha or Krishna, but instead he became conscious of a bright radiance which entered the room, filling it, and he describes what subsequently happened as follows:

"I opened the door to see where it came from, but all was dark outside. I returned inside, and the light increased in intensity and took the form of a globe of light above the ground, and in the light there appeared, not the form I expected, but the living Christ I had counted as dead. To all eternity I shall never forget his glorious and loving face, nor the few words which he spoke: 'Why do you persecute me? See, I have died on the cross for you and for the whole world.' These words were burned into my heart as if by lightning, and I fell on the ground before him. My heart was filled with inexpressible joy and peace, and my whole life was entirely changed. Then the old Sundar Singh died and a new Sundar Singh, to serve the living Christ, was born."

He faced serious opposition from his immediate family and the wider community. After more gentle persuasion failed to change his views, the family and community resorted to severe persecution and even attempted abduction and murder. He came under the protection of Presbyterian missionaries and went to the Church Missionary Society station in Simla. He was baptised on 3 September 1905.

In 1909 he entered St John's Divinity School at Lahore but left without completing the course. He wanted the freedom to speak in churches of different denominations, and continued his ministry as a wandering preacher, but remained a member of the Anglican church all his life. Within a few weeks of his baptism he decided to express his Christian discipleship by adopting the distinctive lifestyle of a *Sadhu*, a holy person who has renounced the worldly life. He adopted the saffron robe and *Sadhu* way of life in fulfilment of the vow made in his early days, that if God would satisfy his quest for inner peace, he would sacrifice all that this world could offer him.

The *Sadhu* ideal is not limited to any one tradition within Hinduism, and many, independent of any allegiance, have chosen to wear the saffron robe and adopt a lifestyle which fits broadly within the Hindu religious way of life. Sundar Singh's appropriation of the *Sadhu* way of life was independent of any existing Hindu religious order, and was an attempt to pursue Christian discipleship in a manner consistent with the *Sadhu* ideal in the Hindu tradition. He was the first Protestant known to have embraced this way of life. It aroused misunderstanding and opposition from two quarters. On the one hand, the Christian community wondered whether the Hindu ideal of renunciation was compatible with a Christian worldview that affirmed the material world. On the other hand, the Hindu community was suspicious that this was a fraudulent attempt to camouflage the Christian message by the adoption of Hindu forms.

Sundar Singh pursued the ministry of an itinerant preacher, travelling across north and south India, Tibet and Nepal. He endured much humiliation and suffered many hardships. His later travels took him to the Far East, England, the United States, Australia and the Middle East. To his deep distress, his integrity was assaulted and his failing health caused him to withdraw to his retreat in Subathu in Himachal Pradesh. Here he gave himself to meditation and writing his devotional books. In April 1929 he set out on his last missionary journey to Tibet, during which he disappeared in mysterious circumstances and was never seen again.

Sundar Singh's sermons and writings are of great value to us, both for their distinctive theological content as well as their widespread and prolonged influence. They are marked by direct simplicity of insights and vividness of expression. His distinctive interpretation of the Christian faith, as embodied in his lifestyle and reflected in his sermons and writings, raised questions on his mystical orientation with little attention paid to a theological evaluation of his teaching. This was mainly related to the *Sadhu* controversy and his adoption of the *Sadhu* way of life. His contribution to the development of Indian Christianity has thus been largely neglected and his approach to other religions almost totally ignored. His fulfilment approach was as an Indian convert to the Christian faith whose access to the innermost chambers of Indian spirituality resulted in the emergence of an original framework for relating the Christian faith to the *bhakti* tradition.

The outstanding characteristic of Sundar Singh's theology is that it is grounded in personal experience. He felt that people do not believe because they are strangers to the experience, but that faith and experience must come first, and understanding will follow. He believed that understanding follows spiritual experience, and that comes through prayer.

Sundar Singh's emphasis on spiritual experience is widely acknowledged. An early analysis of his life and thought identified him as a mystic rather than a philosopher, theologian or scholar. Most commentators locate the roots for his mystical experience in his pre-Christian *bhakti* roots. He clearly affirms the presence of some measure of light from God in Hinduism despite his rejection of Hinduism as a religious system. His mother's religious devotion within the *bhakti* tradition of Hinduism and Sikhism was a huge influence on his spiritual formation. The only other individual who exercised any significant influence on him was Mrs Rebecca Parker, a member of the London Missionary Society. He regarded her as his spiritual mother and closest advisor. She in turn had been influenced by a Protestant missionary theology which had been shaped predominantly by the beliefs of the evangelical awakening in Britain in the eighteenth century.

Sundar Singh had little exposure to any other sustained human influence. He regarded human learning of no avail in enhancing one's knowledge of God, and when asked if he ever read books, replied: "I am reading two books, which I can never, never finish... one is the Holy Bible, and the second is Nature."

This negative attitude to learning, along with his limited knowledge of English and his itinerant lifestyle, ensured that he had very little exposure to western Christian influences. Later in life he seems to have given some attention to reading philosophy, science, mediaeval western spirituality and mysticism. By contrast, the New Testament became a constant source of inspiration and companionship in his travels, and he spent many hours in private Bible reading and meditation.

The two principal influences on Sundar Singh's mystical formation were his pre-conversion Hindu and Sikh *bhakti* formation and his biblical reflection.

Among the various Hindu scriptures he was exposed to in his early years was the Bhagavad Gita, which he had memorised by the age of seven and which had pride of place in his heart. He felt that there was evidence that it had been influenced by the teaching of John's Gospel. His view recognised that it represented an assorted collection of material, but it also reflected an acquaintance with a prevailing school of thought which detected Christian influence in it, and this in some way influenced his mystical orientation.

A further strand of *bhakti* thought which influenced Sundar Singh was the Sikh religion which is essentially a religion of experience. The ultimate purpose of all life and religion is an inward union with God resulting in eternal bliss. Guru Nanak was the founder of Sikhism and the first of the ten Sikh Gurus whose mystical vision was grounded in his understanding of the nature of God as the one eternal, formless creator and sustainer. However humankind is separated from God by an impure heart (*man*) and corrupted by sin (*haumai*) due to the temptations of this world (*maya*) and remains a prisoner to the cycle of transmigration. The gracious initiative (*nadar*) of God (*Guru*) is humankind's only hope for salvation. Nature reveals God's nature to the person who is sensitive to the voice of God mystically uttered within the inner recesses of the human soul. The enlightened one thus comprehends the Word (*Sabad*) of God in the world and in his inner experience. He responds in loving adoration, meditates on the revealed nature and qualities of God, and thus draws nearer to God, finally reaching the supreme bliss of consummate union.

Although some have found little trace of Sikh influence on Sundar Singh's spiritual formation, it may be due to the fact that he emphasised the importance given to Hindu teaching in his home. However, the mediaeval Hindu *bhakti* impulses nourished the Sikh tradition and most commentators regard Sikh and Hindu *bhakti* as having an equal role in his pre-Christian formation. His *bhakti* background functioned as an underlying framework for the development of the fulfilment concept in his understanding.

Sundar Singh echoes a facet of Sikh mystical theology when he speaks of God as ineffable and ultimately incomprehensible in essence, transcending all human categories and powers of expression. The emphasis on God as Truth, the All-True One, resonates deeply with the Sikh view.

The conception of God as love is at the heart of the *bhakti* framework and, for Sundar Singh, God is supremely and above all else perfect, pure, self-giving love.

He made a significant departure from the Sikh *bhakti* in his acceptance of the possibility of an incarnation or *avatara*, a Hindu concept, integral to *Vaishnava bhakti*, that means 'descent' and refers to the material appearance or incarnation of a deity on earth. His pre-Christian *avatara* aspiration was fulfilled in his experience of Christ, seen clearly in his full affirmation of Christ as 'the Word Incarnate', and he does not hesitate to use the term *avatara* to describe the incarnation.

According to Sundar Singh, God is always present in his creation, and every aspect of God's creation, both visible and invisible, in some way reflects the nature and attributes of God. He seems to allow for the place of reason in arriving at the knowledge of God but admits a certain differentiation in this universal knowledge. Those who possess this innate knowledge in a smaller measure require some spiritual insight or illumination by the Holy Spirit.

Sundar Singh's background had also prepared him for the acceptance of the Bible as the authoritative written revelation, for Sikhism gives a high degree of importance to its written scriptures, the Granth Sahib, viewing it as *guru*, the means to divine guidance and as a channel of communication between God and man. His words and practice, however, leave us in little doubt that he regarded the Bible as the divinely revealed word of God.

Sundar Singh's understanding of salvation is strongly conditioned by the *bhakti* mystical quest for union with the divine. Following his conversion, he seems to have been convinced that salvation is not the result of natural human goodness or effort but comes as the free gift of a gracious and merciful God. In his pre-Christian religious consciousness, he understood that the gracious initiative of God in the work of salvation is a crucial theme in Sikhism. In the human quest for salvation there is a point beyond which human understanding cannot proceed. It is at God's gracious initiative (*nadar*) that man receives the gift of illuminating perception (*guru*) through which he understands the need for, and the means of obtaining, salvation. This understanding of the gracious divine initiative most likely conditioned his prayer for a special revelation at the climax of his religious crisis.

In summary, his use of the *bhakti* sources in his framework represented an assorted synthesis of elements specific to the *Vaishnava* and Sikh *bhakti* traditions. There is clear evidence that his conversion experience was conditioned by his pre-Christian *bhakti* consciousness, while his *bhakti* background prepared him for his experience of the Christian faith in a number of ways – for example, his view of God as a loving, personal creator, distinct from and yet immanent in his creation, the acceptance of the possibility of the incarnation, the recognition of the divine authority of the written word, the idea of sin as a moral evil, and the recognition that salvation comes at the gracious initiative of God.

Sundar Singh saw the aspirations of his *bhakti* experience finding their convergence and fulfilment in Christ summarised in his famous and oft-quoted analogy: "Christianity is the fulfilment of Hinduism. Hinduism has been digging channels. Christ is the water to flow through these channels."

He acknowledged that there were many sincere seekers after the truth among the teachers of Hinduism, and many devotees who had received some measure of light. However, he regarded Hinduism as having failed to meet the religious need of India. In his brief discussion of the teachings of the Bhagavad Gita, he contrasts Krishna with Christ at one main point. Whereas Krishna came to save the righteous and destroy sinners, Christ came to save sinners. He likewise found Buddhism inadequate, since the Buddhist vision of Nirvana, the extinction of all desires, denies the reality of man's vital relationship to the created order, and the legitimacy of certain God-given desires essential to life. It results ultimately in the destruction of life rather than salvation. His discussion of Islam focuses essentially on the Qur'anic designation of Christ as 'Ruhallah', the All-Spirit of God, based on which he disputes the Muslim rejection of the divinity of Christ.

Sundar Singh's more extensive discussion of the Christian faith attempts to demonstrate the sufficiency of Christ to satisfy the human spirit's deepest need. He tries to show that the Christian faith is a true, living and satisfying religion which alone enables man to reaches his final destination and moral perfection through mystical communion with God. He does not regard all religions as equally legitimate ways to God, but he views the vision of God in Christ as completing what was lacking in many other religions of the world.

In his book *With and Without Christ*, Sundar Singh compares real life experiences of Christians and non-Christians, distinguishing them as with and without God. He says that Christians and non-Christians are equally the creations of one God. Christians have a true knowledge of God, are being transformed into his likeness and have become heirs of eternal life through Jesus Christ. Non-Christians are those who are walking in the dim light of the truth as they know it, but in choosing to stray away from it, forfeit the blessings that are available in Christ. He recounts real-life encounters with several non-Christians without Christ, highlighting their sense of futility when they failed to find God apart from Christ. Despite the light of truth, followers of different religions are '... without the touch of the living Christ, their lives have no abiding peace and hope', and they are unable to satisfy their deepest spiritual needs by their own natural goodness or human effort.

Sundar Singh speaks of those he calls 'non-Christians with Christ', as those who secretly believe in Christ as their Saviour as well as those more deeply influenced by Christ than by their own religions or teachers. In the latter category, he includes Hindu reformers who, despite their overt antagonism to Christianity, have reinterpreted their ancestral religion in the light of the teachings of Christ. He also focuses on those groups of secret disciples who, not disassociating themselves from their non-Christian environment, still seek to follow Christ in their lives. These secret disciples who have accepted Christ as their Saviour and are baptised, have never publicly identified themselves with the visible organised Church, but worship and serve God in secret.

In justifying the legitimacy of this claim, Sundar Singh insists that the quickening work of the living Christ is not confined to organised churches but is going on among non-Christians, and he shares several testimonies from his own experience of Hindu, Muslim and Sikh 'non-Christians with Christ'. In his view, while a relationship with Christ is indispensable for salvation, identification with the visible Church seems not to be essential.

Sundar Singh acknowledges the presence of a dim measure of the light of truth among the followers of different religions. If honest seekers of all religions live true to the light they already possess, God gives them more light and they will eventually arrive at a full knowledge of God. His view in this regard was significantly conditioned by his deep affection and respect for his mother, who seems to represent for him an archetype of the Christian seeker after truth. In a conversation with the Archbishop of Uppsala, he offers the following description of his mother's religious devotion: "People call us heathen... just fancy! My mother a heathen! If she were alive now, she would certainly be a Christian. But even while she followed her ancestral faith she was so religious that the term 'heathen' makes me smile. She prayed to God, she served God, she loved God, far more warmly and deeply than many Christians..."

He applies essentially the same observation in a broader contrast between the ardent spiritual passion of Indian seekers after truth and his perception of the religious superficiality in many quarters of western Christianity.

"So far as I can see, there are many more people among us in India who lead a spiritual life than in the west, although they do not know or confess Christ. They live truly according to the light which God has given them... Among us in India there are many, many that lead a holy life... the 'heathen' (Indians) do not seek for days or months only, they go on seeking earnestly and anxiously the truth for years at a time... Idol-worshippers seek the truth, but people over here, so far as I can see, seek only pleasure and comfort."

He regards the worship of idols by sincere seekers after truth as representing a limited but authentic encounter with God. Although there is no consoling power in the stone idol, it is useful as 'a means of concentration on God' and may provide divine consolation depending on their measure of faith. He thus concurs closely with Farquhar in his willingness to grant a significant amount of validity to non-Christian religious experience.

Is the encounter with God mediated through non-Christian religious experience essentially continuous or qualitatively different from the experience of God in Christ? Sundar Singh seems to emphasise essential continuity rather than difference when he suggests that there are sincere seekers who may know Christ without knowing his name:

'There are... in India men who live in God without knowing Christ. That is, they do not know his name.'

This is made more explicit when he clarifies that non-Christians who need the fullest light that Christ gives already have some access to the Holy Spirit and to the light of Christ, and the Sun of Righteousness. He is convinced that, because of his infinite grace and mercy, God does not judge an individual based on the correctness of his beliefs; rather, he rewards genuineness in the heart of the sincere seeker by a further revelation of the truth as it really is. He seems to believe that non-Christians will have the opportunity in the after-life to have some partial views corrected and to hold a view of unlimited grace in which very few will be lost and many will be saved. However, he clearly regards non-Christian religions as basically inadequate, rejecting them as systems. His view of salvation must be analysed in the context of its location between two poles. God's concern for the salvation of all humankind, and the decisiveness of Christ in God's plan of salvation. There seems to be a certain degree of ambiguity in his teaching on this. On the one hand, he speaks of judgement in hell in terms that affirm the Church's traditional doctrine of everlasting punishment, and that it is not God who sends sinners to hell; people of their own free will turn their faces away from God. On the other hand, his view of salvation is the conviction that God's incarnation and redemption in Christ constitute the climax of his loving response to man's longing for communion with him: "We in India... already know that God is good. But we did not know that he was so good that Christ was willing to die for us. There is much that is beautiful in Hinduism, but the highest light comes from Christ."

Sundar Singh was acutely conscious of the importance of indigenisation and the need for incorporating harmonious elements of his pre-Christian religion tradition within the interpretation of the Christian faith. In a famous illustration, he relates the incident in which a high-caste Brahmin collapsed on a station platform on account of extreme heat and thirst, but refused a drink of water offered to him in a china cup. When water was brought to him in his own brass vessel, he accepted it gladly. His application of this incident is perhaps one of his best-known sayings: "Indians greatly need the Water of Life but they do not want it in European vessels."

Although he did not formally become involved in any organisation of social action, Sundar Singh was, for a short period, involved in serving those stricken with smallpox and plague as well as caring for those stricken with leprosy and the physically handicapped. His love for humankind and ideal of joyful service was for the most part expressed through his evangelistic and missionary endeavours, but he certainly did not believe that his ascetic practices earned his salvation.

There are the marks of yogic influence in several aspects of Sundar Singh's religious practice. Yoga as a system of physical and mental discipline is usually an integral part of the ascetic practice of a *Sadhu*, and Sundar Singh possessed, to a remarkable degree, the yogic ability to bear the bodily wants of hunger and thirst, heat and cold. In the years before his conversion, certain techniques of yoga significantly conditioned his approach to prayer and meditation. He never seems to have given up the discipline of meditation he learned through Yoga. Although he found these practices unsatisfying when he became a Christian, he did not abandon them altogether, but rather sought to transform them and use them in Christ's service.

Meditation played an important role in his pre-Christian religious formation. Yoga meditation techniques appear to have been a means of entrance into his mystical experience, often characterised by ecstasy and accompanied by visions. These helped him persevere with the *Sadhu* lifestyle. While he regarded these ecstatic experiences as gifts and valued them highly, he did not believe that they should be sought after or induced. It was his employment of the yogic technique in his practice of meditation that helped mediate his experience of the Christian vision of union with Christ.

Sundar Singh manifests a tension between differing views in his attitude towards Hinduism. On the one hand, he rejects Hinduism as a system, regarding it as having failed to meet the religious needs of India. On the other hand, he is sympathetic with the basic religious impulses of Hinduism, in particular the *bhakti* quest for union with

God. He felt that in the progressive journey of the human race towards the truth, sincere seekers are headed in the right direction, and will be divinely guided towards a perfect apprehension of reality which they encounter in the risen Christ. He sometimes makes the Hindu traditions serve as an Old Testament to the Hindu community in relation to the Christian faith, and compares the role of the ancient Hindu *rishis* (seers and sages) who served as mediators of the law in the Indian context, to Moses' role in mediating the Law of God to the Jews.

In one instance, he recounts the testimony of a Hindu *pandit* [priest], who had been convinced, by two Christian *Sadhus*, that Christ was the sinless incarnation promised in the Hindu scriptures, and the only Saviour. In the explanation, they compare the function of the law of *karma* in the Hindu religion to the law in other religions. There are sources which suggest that Sundar Singh may also have shared Banerjea's conviction that Jesus was the fulfilment of the Vedic figure of *Prajapati*, who sacrificed his life for the sins of the world, but the evidence does not indicate whether this was due to any acquaintance with Banerjea's work or whether he had arrived at this view independently.

What then is the value of the partial and provisional knowledge of God that Hindus have access to apart from Christ? Sundar Singh, the mystic rather than the theologian, has little to say regarding the objective knowledge of God in other religions. On the other hand, he is vitally concerned about their subjective value in testifying to the fervent desire within the human heart for mystical union with God.

Sundar Singh takes the revelation of God in nature very seriously. The created world is a reflection of God's nature and attributes, and as part of this reflection of God in nature, man is innately endowed with a capacity of mystical knowledge which enables him to experience God in the natural order. As wonderful as the revelation of God in the natural order is, his revelation in the heart of man is much greater. It enables men to discern God's presence in the world, and creates a desire for more of God's presence in a heart positively attuned to him.

The Logos-Christ of Sundar Singh's mystical experience has some agreement with Sen's ideas. Christ is the centre of both their religious experiences, and the historical Jesus appears to be of less consequence than the Logos-Christ. The focus of Sen's experience was the Spirit-Christ or the all-pervading Logos-Christ. For Sundar Singh, it was the risen, living, inward Christ. Both agree with the early Church Fathers in owning truth wherever it may be found as God's truth, and seeing traces of God's revelation and the Logos-Christ in non-Christian religious experience, philosophy, science, poetry and art. The various fragments of truth are brought together in Christ in whom alone the Logos-light is manifested in full measure.

Sundar Singh's approach departs from Sen's in his clear emphasis on the Christ of history.

In this respect, his view resonates more deeply with that of the Logos theology of the early Church Fathers. With them, he recognises the Logos as the agent and sustainer of the created world, present and active in it since the time of creation, and sees the illuminating action of the Logos in glimpses of revelation, faith and grace, apart from his specific revelation in Christ. But for Sundar Singh, the Logos-Light was most sharply focused in the incarnate Christ of history, the living, resurrected Lord of Christian faith:

"The Wise Men followed the star of Bethlehem. But when they reached Bethlehem, they no longer needed the star, for they had found Christ, the Sun of Righteousness. When the sun rises, the stars lose their radiance... In India we have many genuine truth-seekers who faithfully follow their star, but it is only starlight which guides them. But you Christians have the glory of the sun... Hinduism and Buddhism have dug canals, but they had no living water to fill them. In this sense, I was prepared to receive the living water from Christ. Christianity is the fulfilment of Hinduism."

Sundar Singh's theological intentions are unmistakable. The pre-Christian light of the Logos is only starlight, in contrast to the glorious light of Christ the Sun of Righteousness before whose glory the starlight fades. The Logos-light only prepares channels, and is distinguished from the light the living Christ brings as the living water which must flow through these channels.

Sundar Singh was a mystic saint and evangelist rather than a thinker. His theology has been perceived as simplistic and elementary by some and given cursory treatment, while others have heralded him as an original, creative and mystical genius.

A Summary of the Contributions of Farquhar, Banerjea and Sundar Singh to Fulfilment Thought

While this study looks at the fulfilment stream that emerged in the experience and reflection of converts to the Christian faith during the pre-Independence period, it exposes the need for further insight in three areas. First, confirmation of its claim that the Hindu tradition can be seen as a pathway to Christ. Secondly, adoption of an appropriate theological device for affirming Hindu-Christian continuity. Thirdly, formation of an adequate Christology that responds positively to certain aspects of the Hindu tradition while affirming the central claims of the Christian faith.

Farquhar's fulfilment approach was forged in response to the prevailing perception of Christianity as a denationalising influence, and Christian mission as a destructive invasion of traditional Indian culture. His apologetic attempted to assert the relevance of Christ to India against the charge that the Christian message was an assault on the spirit of nationalism. This led him to a serious investigation of the Hindu religious sources in search of a way for affirming continuity between the Christian faith and the Hindu tradition. His approach sought to distinguish between what was applicable universally to all peoples in the Christian Gospel, and what was not, and so to provide a basis for distinguishing the evangelistic mandate of sharing the message of Christ from the imperialistic trappings that often accompanied it.

Most of the Indian fulfilment contributions were forged in response to the common rejection of the Christian message, based not on religious or philosophical grounds, but on the perception of it being foreign. Although Sen, Goreh, Upadhyay and Tilak drew their insights from different sources, they were all concerned with refuting the charges of cultural foreignness and the irrelevance of the Christian faith. Sen speaks of Christ coming to India as an 'Asiatic in race' and 'Hindu in faith', and despite his deep attraction to Christ, remained within the Hindu fold all his life.

Goreh consciously resisted western influence upon his traditional culture and lifestyle, and despite the influence of rationalism and western orthodoxy, confirmed the presence of divine light within the Hindu tradition. Similarly, Upadhyay's lifelong quest for a Hindu Catholic theology and identity resulted in him remaining a patriotic nationalist all his life.

Tilak claimed that his quest for an ideal religion that would provide the spiritual foundation for a prosperous India led him to Christ. His deep love for his Hindu spiritual heritage and lifelong attempts to free the person and message of Christ from western cultural forms, led him eventually to launch a culturally indigenous Christian movement.

The same impulse is found in Banerjea and Sundar Singh. Banerjea devoted a significant opening segment of *Dialogues* to a series of arguments countering the Hindu opposition to Christianity as a foreign religion, destructive to the Indian way of life. The ultimate objective of *Arian Witness* was to refute the charge that Christianity was a foreign religion and that Hindu converts to Christianity betrayed their ancestral faith. His overriding concern seems to have been to redeem the Christian faith from the charge of foreignness and to demonstrate that Hindu converts could remain loyal to their ancestral culture even as disciples of Christ.

In Sundar Singh, the impulse is expressed most clearly in his famous phrase saying: "Indians greatly need the Water of Life but they do not want it in European vessels." Although implied in his attempt to draw lines of continuity between the Hindu tradition and the Christian faith, this principle is most explicitly applied in his conscious adoption of the *Sadhu* lifestyle, not just as an evangelist but as an attempt to represent the Christian Gospel in a form of living expression that represented the highest ideals of Hindu religion.

Thus, like Farquhar, Indian thinkers go to great lengths to distinguish the theological task from the imperialistic project with which the Christian mission was frequently confused.

As far as their theology goes, Sen, although not a Christian, sees the Hindu scriptures as pointing prophetically to the coming Christ. Upadhyay felt that in the idea of Logos fulfilment, natural religion reaches its highest form of expression in the Vedantic conception of Brahman as *Saccidananda*, the ultimate, unchanging reality.

Tilak regarded the Hindu devotional literature and the writings of the *bhakti* poet-saints as serving as an Old Testament for Hindus in India. His own spiritual journey convinced him that the Hindu scriptures anticipated and prepared Hindus to receive the message of Christ.

Banerjea focuses on objective pointers to Christ in the Vedic texts, whereas Sundar Singh sees a more subjective testimony to Christ in

Hindu religious experience. Banerjea was convinced that the Vedas offered greater potential for providing a meeting-point between Hinduism and Christianity than later philosophical schools. He discovered fragments of truth in them which seemed to affirm what he considered the essentials of the Christian faith. He saw a prophetic prediction of Christ in the recognition of sacrifice as the great remedy for sins in certain Vedic texts, and more specifically in the Vedic self-sacrificing divine figure of *Prajapati*.

Sundar Singh's view of the anticipation of Christ within the Hindu tradition is aptly summarised in his metaphor of Christ as the water of life that flow through the channels created by Hinduism, and that the impulse of the union with God, within the mystical consciousness, constituted a preparation for Christ.

The Jewish Christian impulse to affirm the continuity of Jesus' person and message with the Jewish scriptures parallels the inbuilt impulse of Indian Christian converts to affirm continuity in relation to the Hindu tradition. This New Testament promise-fulfilment approach has served as a model for subsequent approaches to the Christological reading of non-Christian religious texts.

Paul's address to the Greeks at Athens in Acts 17 offers an illustration of the Christian use of non-Christian texts outside the Jewish context. Paul avoids any direct reference to the Old Testament, but makes use of several concepts of distinctly pagan origin. The first is the inscription on the altar 'to the unknown God', probably one of several such altars in Athens integral to the religious consciousness of the Athenians. It served as a point of contact which Paul used to launch his speech. Although the ignorance, rather than the worship, was underlined, Paul clearly intended to convey that he was now making known to them this 'unknown God' that they worshipped in ignorance.

The phrase 'in him we live and move and have our being' is a reference traced back to the to the sixth century BC poet Epimenides, the Cretan. And, 'for we are indeed his offspring' in Acts 17 v 28 is a citation from a third century BC poet, Aratus of Cilicia. A further reference to pagan sources is the allusion to Stoic philosophy that Paul uses in Acts 17 v 27 in the expression, 'Men should seek God, in the hope that they might feel after him.'

Paul's desire to affirm continuity, together with his recognition of elements of truth in Gentile religion, does not make him overlook elements of discontinuity. In Paul's view, the religion of the Gentiles represented a mixture of truth and error. His reference to 'the unknown God' was designed to convey the fact that although the quest expressed in the worship of the Athenians was legitimate, their mode of worship as polytheistic idolatry was not. Paul's use of non-Christian texts was complemented by his assertion of the transcendent elements of Christian newness.

Indian converts such as Banerjea, Sundar Singh and others are in a position comparable with the early Jewish Christians and Gentile converts who could legitimately claim the right to interpret their ancestral religious tradition from the perspective of their Christian experience. This prerogative became a duty in the light of the need to justify their conversion to Christ against the charge of national and religious apostasy.

When John used the term Logos, it undoubtedly aroused certain specific religious and philosophical associations among his readers, whatever their background. For Jew and Gentile alike, the Logos represented the ruling fact of the universe, the self-expression of God and the starting-point of all things. It was a term that would be widely recognised by his Gentile audience, and strike familiar chords among Greek readers in particular. Based on the prevailing understanding of the Logos as the self-expression of ultimate divinity, giving unity to the whole cosmos, John as the author of the fourth Gospel and some early patristic writers employed it in communicating the truth of the incarnation to the Greek world, and the Church endorsed the specific Christian significance assigned to this term.

Like the Logos concept, the *Prajapati* ideal is originally rooted outside the Christian tradition, possessing distinct religious and philosophical connotations within the Hindu tradition. In both instances, while some nuances of meaning may be remote from the original meaning, other senses overlap with the idea being conveyed. The early Christian theologians nevertheless use the term Logos in a way that was continuous with its prior significance, and yet they extended its meaning, making it do something new in order to express a Christian reality. Banerjea's similar strategy with the concept of *Prajapati* can be justified from John's approach. One difference however is that the term *Prajapati* is not as widely known, nor its connotations as widely understood in the Indian context, as the term Logos was in the first century Near Eastern context.

Conclusion

This study has set out to detail the development of fulfilment theology in the pre-Independence period in India, focusing especially on the views of Banerjea and Sundar Singh. It explores the relationship between Christian truths and the evidence in non-Christian religious tradition of the universal revealing and redemptive action of God towards all humankind.

Both men confirm that there are elements in the Hindu tradition and experience that can lead earnest seekers to Christ. The understanding of this was based on a consideration of the elements of continuity and discontinuity comparable with the Jewish Christian reading of the Jewish scriptures and the use of non-Christian texts in the New Testament apostolic preaching.

Furthermore, they both suggest a theological basis for affirming continuity between the Christian revelation and aspects of the Hindu religious tradition. Although their perspectives are distinct, they are not incompatible and may be incorporated within a broader Trinitarian scheme of progressive, differentiated and complementary divine revelation. They also provide material for a theologically logical Christology to undergird the fulfilment proposal. Banerjea's original conception of the creator-redeemer figure of *Prajapati* provides a useful objective complement to Sundar Singh's rudimentary Logos theology, both ideas resonating deeply with New Testament and patristic impulses.

Fulfilment theology received firm endorsement from the Protestant missionary community at Edinburgh in 1910 and continued to exercise influence until the Tambaram missionary conference of 1938 when it was buried under the weight of a broadside from Hendrik Kraemer, a missiologist and leading figure in the ecumenical movement from the Dutch Reformed Church in the Netherlands. He emphasised the uniqueness of the Christian Gospel and its essential discontinuity with any aspect of human religion. This, together with further polarisation at the World Council of Churches' Assembly in Nairobi in 1975, and at the Vancouver Assembly in 1983, led to the marginalisation of the fulfilment tradition in Protestant circles and its decline in the latter part of the twentieth century.

Another reason for its decline was the altered composition of the Indian church. The early and middle years of the nineteenth century witnessed the conversion of a significant number of high-caste Brahmins. Thus Banerjea, Goreh, Upadhyay and Tilak represented a class of educated Brahmin convert thoroughly versed in Sanskrit, with an intimate grasp of the Hindu religious text – and the Christian mission to those of a higher caste in the years following the Hindu renaissance required serious engagement with the sources of Hindu tradition. The middle years of the nineteenth century saw Christianity increasingly involved with the lower castes and Dalit communities with the rapid growth of the Christian Church among the more backward tribal groups. Subsequent generations saw fewer converts from the high-caste Hindu community, from within which the fulfilment tradition had earlier emerged and had its primary appeal.

A third factor that adversely affected the influence of the fulfilment approach in India in the twentieth century was the socio-economic context following Independence. Issues of Christians and nationalism, nation-building and church union, took precedence over the question of the relationship of Christianity with other faiths.

Subsequently, the predominantly Dalit composition of the Church has brought issues of Dalit identity, theology and spirituality to the fore. When the issue of religious pluralism eventually returned to the Indian theological agenda in the closing decades of the twentieth century, it began to be addressed with little reference to the earlier fulfilment tradition.

As responsible stewards of the Christian Gospel, it is important to revisit this Indian tradition of fulfilment theology. The anti-religions posture of the nineteenth century Protestant missionary tradition continues to be expressed within some quarters of evangelical Protestantism today. Representatives of this attitude are passionately committed to the absolute truthfulness of the Gospel of Christ, but often adopt a prejudiced ideological stance against other religions.

But there are other pioneers whose fulfilment views should be examined in detail to refine and, if necessary, correct the conclusions represented in this book. There is also a need for the development of a Christian hermeneutic or a study of non-Christian texts to provide further help and discussion in this area. While this study has suggested a broad theological framework for a Christian approach to the textual sources and religious experiences of people of other faiths, Christians need more detailed guidelines on how to read the religious texts of other faiths.

It is important that the conclusions of this study are tested in the light of the living experience of Hindu followers of Christ. If our conclusions are confirmed, it would not only strengthen the broader case for fulfilment theology, it would also help alleviate some of the Hindu nationalist apprehensions regarding Christian mission. Christian mission need never envisage the destruction of Hinduism, or any other religion or worldview, which has a right to exist if it continues to meet the needs of people in our world. Fulfilment theology enables the church to be faithful to its stewardship of the story of God's decisive word and action in Christ, while demonstrating that there is nothing intrinsic to Christian faith that threatens the future of any indigenous cultural heritage. It can provide a basis for the Church to co-operate with people of all faiths in furthering the kingdom purpose of God for a better world, free of poverty, injustice and strife, challenging what is deficient and affirming what is of value in every religion, including Christianity as a religious system.

Further Reading

For those who wish to explore this area further, Ivan Satyavrata's unedited thesis is available from Regnum Books International and contains an extensive bibliography.

St. Philip and St. James Church
Woodstock Road
Oxford, OX2 6HR, UK
www.ocms.ac.uk/regnum

Sharpe, E.J., *Faith Meets Faith: Some Christian Attitudes to Hinduism in the Nineteenth and Twentieth Centuries*. London: SCM Press Ltd, 1977.

Richard, H.L., *A Survey of Protestant Evangelistic Efforts among High Caste Hindus in the Twentieth Century*, in *Missiology: An International Review*, 25/4 (1997): 419-45.

Netland, Harold, *Encountering Religious Pluralism: The Challenge to Christian Faith and Mission.*' Leicester, UK: Apollos/IVP, 2001.

Wright, Chris, *The Uniqueness of Jesus*. Grand Rapids, MI: Monarch, 2001.

D'Costa, Gavin, Knitter, Paul F. and Strange, Daniel, *Only One Way?: Three Christian Responses to the Uniqueness of Christ in a Religiously Pluralist World.* London: SCM Press, 2011.

Regnum Mini-Books

Corruption and the Church | Martin Allaby

How do Christians in the global south see the relationship between the church and corruption? This book summarises the views of 101 leaders of churches, Christian faith-based organisations and anti-corruption organisations, as told during in-depth interviews with the author. Capturing voices from across three continents, this summary and analysis of their views makes for some uncomfortable reading, but suggests some constructive ways forward.

Deliver Us from Evil | Roberto Laver

Christians have been largely silent on the issue of corruption. Roberto Laver has been one of the few voices of the Christian community calling for the church to stand up and address this issue. Laver's scholarship undergirded by his faith and concern for the poor and marginalized, gives Christians a compelling wake-up call to confront this scourge. In so doing, he takes a big step toward filling a conspicuous gap in the literature of mission study and practice.

Confronting Corruption | Richard King

Corruption blights the lives of countless people around our world. The purpose of this book is to transform attitudes and behaviours of Christians who live in societies where corrupt behaviour is a fact of life and to do this by letting the Bible, as God's word, speak. The book is intended to be used for weekly reading by pastors at church services to remind congregations that corruption has no place in Christian life, as a resource for Bible colleges in training pastors/church workers and for small group Bible study.

Regnum Mini-Books

Unity & Reconciliation in Rwanda | S Cyuma

In the last ten years of the 20th century, the world was twice confronted with unbelievable news from Africa. Can we compare the situation in South Africa with that in Rwanda? Can Rwandan leaders draw lessons from the peace process in South Africa? These are some of the questions that this publication addresses.

Bridging the Cultural Gap | Ole Kirchheiner

This is an abridged version of Ole Kirchheiner's Regnum book, Culture and Christianity Negotiated in Hindu Society. Through an examination of the Nepali church the study pays special attention to the way ordinary Christians have been able to settle social and religious issues to live and work together with the traditional religious people of Nepal, and maintain a good family life.

Seeking Reconciliation | Peter Rowan

With a history of racial violence and in recent years, low-level ethnic tensions, the themes of peaceful coexistence and social harmony are recurring ones in the discourse of Malaysian society. In such a context, this book looks at the role of the church as a reconciling agent, arguing that a reconciling presence within a divided society necessitates an ethos of peacemaking. Such an ethos is created and sustained when Christians understand that their identity has been transformed in Jesus Christ.